DESTINED FOR STARDOM

"Peter Monroy Story"

Steven K Craig

Copyright © 2016, Steven Craig. All rights reserved.

This book, or parts thereof, may not be reproduced in any form without the written permission from the author; exceptions are made for brief excerpts used in publication reviews.

Printed in the United States of America

ISBN-10: 0692585710
ISBN-13: 978-0692585719

10 9 8 7 6 5 4 3 2

Empire Publishing

www.empire-publishing.com

A special "Thank You" and photo credit goes to:

Linda Saldana (60, 61, 63, 69, 82)

Caroline Esparza-Pena (44)

Contents

Author Introduction 1

Peter Monroy 21

Spandex Nation 64

Monroy 70

*Dedicated to all the fans of Hair Metal
and the MonRockers worldwide*

Author Introduction

Many people in my age group (born 1968 or earlier) remember the fierce passion excitement, ferocity, sensual pleasure and glamour during the explosive era of Heavy Metal and Hair Metal throughout the 1980's. Mtv was born and actually broadcast music videos back then that gave exposure to the metal spiked, leather and lace clad after dark guitar warriors. It was an era where music was more than something merely listened to on the radio – it was a lifestyle. It was truly a "Decade of Decadence" as bands experimented with sound, guitar riffs, imagery and theatrics vying to become rock and roll superstars, which would launch them out of the clubs on the Sunset Strip and into large arenas. Back then, becoming a rock and roll superstar meant fame, fortune and girls... lots of girls! Obtaining those consumed many hormone overloaded young boy's dreams and fantasies, but then, as we know now, it all came with a hefty price tag.

The music of the 1980's (heavy metal, alternative rock and Pop) molded an entire generation, shaped a new culture and influenced many generations afterwards. The music industry flourished as never before – and never will again. Heavy Metal branched out in many directions so quickly that new sub-genre titles were dubbed almost daily. Heavy Metal covered the full spectrum, from the dark side with black leather, spikes and pentagrams to bright colors, big hair, lace and lipstick. The music ranged from hardcore aggressive thrash to some of the best power ballads ever written. In the overall scope of it, the things that took place during that time have become legendary and will be talked about and written about in history books for many years to come.

I was there to see the beginning as it took place and was part of it throughout its entire duration, which explains my deep love for that time period and genre of music. At twenty years old, when my former high school classmates were either in college or still trying to figure out what they were going to do with their lives, I owned and operated a music production company. What I did was host shows at nightclubs and venues under the moniker of SC Productions. I hired bands to fill the roster for specific shows and eventually managed a few of them through my new company Platinum Management & Direction.

At the time, nightclub bands were performing progressive rock in the vein of Journey and Rush because it was popular in the mainstream. However, behind the scene a new genre of music was forming as the New Wave of British Heavy Metal was sweeping through the underground of the United States. Bands such as Judas Priest, Iron Maiden, the Scorpions and the more commercially viable Def Leppard were making headway and building a massive ever growing fan base in America. Following the trail of Priest, Maiden and Scorpions as they paved the way reminiscent of a brutal bulldozer hell bent on domination, bands in the murky trenches of the United Kingdom such as Tank, Witchfinder General, Saxon, Accept, Diamond Head, Raven Angel Witch, Motorhead and Venom were on the rise and making an impact. The albums by the bands mentioned above could only be found in the import section at record stores. I remember when Judas Priest's "Sad Wings of Destiny" was only available as an import. That record was a rare gem when it made its way to the US, but it was only discovered by those that dared to throw out cash seeking something new that was not heard of nor available through distribution on a US label. Most of the time, a record by an unknown group was disappointing and a total waste of money, but every now and then, one would surface that would light a fire inside and make the eardrums bleed from cranking the stereo up to max volume.

The influence of these pioneering bands that had crossed the Atlantic Ocean, along with the popularity of the innovative earlier guitar wizardry of Eddie Van Halen and Randy Rhoades, began to surface on the local level in Los Angeles. Most of the newly formed bands performed at backyard parties because the clubs would not book the new and heavy style o music for shows, and record companies wanted nothing to do with them. At that time, Motley Crue was gaining momentum with the re-release of their self-produced first album "Too Fast for Love." The album garnished attention due to the photograph of the band with bigger than normal hair. Some believe Motley Crue gave birth to Hair Metal, but that is far from the truth. Before Motley Crue, in the late 1970's there was a local band in Los Angeles that was slated to become superstars. They had the catchy riffs, big hair, glitter and the stage presence of true rock stars. Even after all the years that have gone by, I still remember them singing, "We want to make you sweat. We want to get you wet." That band was Wolfgang.... who later became Autograph and produced the hit single "Turn up the Radio".

I was producing a July 4th (1982) show at the Woodstock Concert Theatre in Anaheim, California and needed a band to fill the fourth slot for the night. The girlfriend of the bass player for one of the bands I was managing told me about a local cover band that played

Heavy Metal and got me their phone number. The spandex-clad band did mostly cover tunes from the Scorpions, AC/DC, Judas Priest and Iron Maiden, along with about five original songs. I saw something I liked in the band, and after that night, I closed SC Productions and began working exclusively with them. I helped create their image, influenced their direction and sound. Along with managing and public relations, I created the logo and stage show. That band is now well known worldwide as the infamous Slayer.

In the beginning, we had a difficult time getting good shows because there were only a handful of Metal bands in the Los Angeles area and a minuscule fan base. We mainly performed in Orange County clubs because the nightclubs in Los Angeles on the Sunset Strip such as Gazzarri's would only book us at 10 pm on a weeknight. Eventually, after the scene exploded, it didn't matter what night bands were booked because the clubs were full of enthusiastic Metal fans any night of the week. However, at this time, we had no choice but to perform with groups in the progressive rock or alternative rock vein. Slayer and Metallica, along with Leatherwolf came out of the garage and into the club scene at the same time.

A&R (artists and repertoire) people wanted nothing to do with Metal bands, and no one could get signed to a record deal. We were all told that Heavy Metal died with Blue Cheer (the first heavy metal band) in the early 70's, and none of us would ever sell a record, but a few entrepreneurs who were Metal fans injected life into the metal embryo that was lying dormant. Brian Slagel, a record store owner, put together and released a compilation album of local metal bands. Metal Massacre was the first in a series of compilation albums that would help launch the careers of many local Heavy Metal bands, including Slayer. The first album included bands such as Ratt, Steeler (with Ron Keel and Yngwie Malmsteen), Malice, Bitch, Black and Blue (second edition) and Metallica.

Even though there was a fierce competition between the local bands, there was also a surprising camaraderie between them as well, and they supported each other through the process of busting into the mainstream. I remember one night in particular when Ratt was playing at Radio City that was located next door to the Woodstock Concert Theatre. The stages were literally back to back with only a wall separating them. Slayer was playing to a full house and I walked over to check out Ratt. I was shocked to see that there were only 17 people in the crowd to watch them perform. At that time, I didn't think Ratt stood a chance of ever achieving any success. I also remember the band members from Great White (Dante Fox) showing up to see Slayer and playing pool in the back. If you were in a popular band that played in Los Angeles, you never had to pay admission to the clubs, so if you weren't playing, you were watching another band perform.

Then the big break came that would open the doors that were virtually sealed shut until then. Quiet Riot released Metal Health, and their first single "Bang Your Head" made its way into regular rotation on Mtv. "Bang Your Head" was a popular phrase used by Metal fans for rapidly bobbing one's head up and down to coincide with the aggressive music, and now the outside world was introduced to it. The doors were not just opened for Metal bands... they were blown apart into kindling and set ablaze.

Hardcore metal bands donning black leather and metal spikes were a novelty and not taken seriously by record companies. They presumed these bands would not have any selling power. But as the scene grew, the genre branched out in many directions. What is now dubbed as Hair Metal was born and hit the mainstream with a huge bang. The hair got bigger, men began to wear makeup, clothes consisted of bright colors adorned with lace and jewels, and rock anthems for the time period were written about sex, love, heartbreak, partying and living life to its fullest. The guys were beautiful and girls flocked in droves to the nightclubs dressed to kill wearing skimpy, sexy, slutty attire, which in turn, brought more males to the shows. The Los Angeles club scene was on fire and the nightclubs were filled to max capacity. Bands such as Poison, Dokken, Ratt, W.A.S.P, Donte Fox (before changing their name to Great White), Armored Saint, Lizzy Borden Guns and Roses and Slayer were packing the houses. Finally, the record companies had to take notice and started signing any band that could pack a club, especially the Country Club in Reseda.

Overnight, the Sunset Strip became the breeding ground for a long list of bands that would become superstars. Hundreds of Heavy/Hair Metal bands went on to accomplish major commercial success.

None of us at the time ever thought that what we were doing would stand the test of time and continue on for many years, let alone, several decades nor would we have imagined that a number of generations later it would reemerge through the fascination of the youth of today.

Then in the early 90's, out of the gutter arose "Grunge" which abruptly killed the long-running party. The new form music was a backlash of the glamorous partying pretty boys and became about self-loathing, suicide and hatred. The pretty boys were replaced with dirty, disturbed social rejects wearing clothes that looked as if they were acquired by rummaging through digging in a trash dumpster.

The music that dominated the airwaves for over a decade died a sudden tragic death. It didn't even get a proper burial and became the butt of a joke for some time by a disgruntled generation which referred to it as "Fag Rock". The definition of "Fag Rock" is, "music that depicts men with "big hair" which uses scantily clad women dancing in videos." All I have to say about that is, "And the problem with that is what? Is someone jealous?" This reminds me of a funny story.

I was partying it up pretty hard at Joshua's Parlor in Garden Grove, Ca which was a hot spot for local bands to hang out. Late one night after closing, we went for a stroll down Huntington Beach pier. I was dressed in full-blown glam garb. Seriously... half of what I was wearing came from a woman's clothing store. I had lace trailers hanging off my overly wide white belt, ruffled shirt similar to the one Prince wore in Purple Rain, a long black jacket adorned with silver jewelry and lace-up leather pants. My long blonde hair was teased and sprayed with Super Hold Aqua Net hairspray to hold it in place high above my head. To complete the look, I had on black eyeliner and lipstick. As we were walking to the end of the pier, five guys were coming towards us. I had a feeling there would be trouble. As they approached, they began to mouth off with comments such as, "Check out the faggot." Faggot? Really? They continued with a barrage of insults. When we got almost face to face, one guy looked at me, and once again, called me a Faggot. I was baffled as I looked at them with their hate-filled expressions and dressed in tattered clothes. Clutched in my right arm was an extremely beautiful blonde girl wearing fishnets and a black leather mini-skirt. My left arm was wrapped around a brunette wearing a small red dress that clung tight to her hot body and even more strikingly beautiful than the blonde. I couldn't refrain, even with the possibility of getting my ass kicked by five guys, and blurted out, "Who are you calling a faggot? You see these two sexy women with me? I'm taking them home with me, and I'm going to have sex mind-blowing with both of them." I hesitated for a moment and then asked, "Where are your women? All I see is a sausage factory. Are you all headed home for a circle jerk?" I don't know why, but that shut them down and we walk through them without another word coming out of their mouths.

Kids today have heard the stories of a legendary era when the music was all about having "Nothing but a good time" and they are yearning for new wave of it to emerge from the ashes so they too can experience its glitter glory. Many have been raised on this genre of music due to the undying love for it by their parents. It makes complete sense that the kids are leaning towards this style of music. Most music of the past few decades are full of hate, bigotry, self-love, doom and gloom, and some of it just plain ridiculous. The music of the 80's was about love, sex, rock & roll all night and party every day. It was about looking spectacular and feeling magnificent.

Hair Metal vanished for a very long time. I remember the most horrible of days when the world famous metal radio station KNAC in Los Angeles went off the air. The last song to be played on KNAC was Metallica's "Fade to Black". At 1:59 p.m. on February 15th 1995, KNAC went off the air and was switched to a Spanish-language music format. This was the last nail in the coffin for Heavy/Hair Metal.

Afterwards, over the span of a few decades, hair metal fans had to get their fix by listening to old recordings, watching old video clip and just fondly reminisce about the glory days of spandex and hair spray.

But now Heavy/Hair Metal is making a comeback! People are tired of the meaningless music today that has no soul, that is, if you want to classify techno or pre-recorded computer generated tracks with vocalists that use auto-tune as music. People want to have their spirits raised, feel exceptionally good inside– and once again, rock and roll all night and party every day.

Many of the bands from that golden era have resurfaced and are trying to make a comeback, but most are unable to produce new music with the same flair and feeling as they once did.

Enter the 80's Tribute bands. These bands have been able to reproduce the excitement, energy, look and feel that was felt on the Sunset Strip circa 1983 – 1989.

It began with Steel Panther – a musically talented band that over exaggerates the nuances of the original bands and adds comedic overtones to their routine. The audience, young and old, eats it up like a hungry pack of wolves with fists stretched up in the air flying the "long live rock and roll" devil horns to show their approval.

Present day, in Las Vegas, Nevada, a new band named Spandex Nation has Fremont Street ablaze every Friday, Saturday and Sunday night by playing to thousands of starving 80's fans from around the world. This ensemble of highly talented musicians donning long flowing wigs, spandex, leather and spikes blast through four hours of music highlighting the golden era music when the women were outrageously sexy and the men were sometimes prettier than the girls; an era when big hair reigned supreme, stock in Aqua Net Super-hold hairspray was higher than General Motors, and mascara, leather, and lace was worn by both men and women.

The first time I saw Spandex Nation at the main stage on Fremont Street in Las Vegas I became an instant fan. It's a rather strange feeling being a fan of an 80's Metal cover band since I was there at the heart of the Sunset Strip during the time the bands that wrote and performed the original songs were getting signed and breaking it into the big time of commercial success. It's reminiscent of the well-known phrase, "The teacher has become the student."

I've frequented Fremont Street a lot in the past, but mostly during the week. Late one winter Saturday night, my girlfriend Frances and I decided to go there. We walked out of Binnion's Casino and immediately I was drawn to the music my ears and mind tuned into off in the distance. I was shocked to hear a band playing Ratt's "Lay It Down" and had to make my way to where it was coming from. The first night seeing Spandex Nation was an orgasmic rush that had me salivating as I re-experienced my youth through each song they performed. Great memories arose through the playlist that

I could have put together myself from old school Hair Metal favorites. I felt fully alive hearing my favorite music played live once again to an almost flawless perfection. I knew right away that this group wasn't a mere ensemble of garage band players, these four guys are highly skilled musicians with each member having an impressive background in music.

From the crowd, I made my first connection with vocalist Peter Monroy as he was performing. I held up my phone in the air to video the band as they blazed through a flawless rendition of Queensryche's "Queen of the Ryche" During the song, Peter lost focus when he flubbed the lyrics, When the song was over, he announced, "I looked out into the crowd and saw this Rocker Dude recording a video, and I thought that I better bring my A-Game because this will end up on Youtube with a critic by him. I was concentrating so hard on giving a great performance that I was getting flustered. I tried to focus on the sexy girls in the front and then I forgot the lyrics." Sure enough, I did post it on YouTube as an eight-part series entitled, "Journey to Spandex Nation".

I was further impressed by the band when they performed the live version with the intro to Dokken's "Alone Again" from Beast in the East and Motley Crue's "Home Sweet Home", where my girlfriend Frances and I went old school by holding lighters in the air. Peter smiled and gave us thumbs up when he saw us.

After several weeks of seeing the band play live, Frances and I were hanging around the stage afterward when a scruffy little guy came out from backstage and waved at us. He's not very tall with short hair that is spiked up in the center. I didn't recognize him at first. I thought he was part of the crew, and then I realized it was Peter without his wig on. I walked over to him to say hello and was pleased to meet such a soft spoken genuinely kind man. He had seen my first YouTube video where Frances and I went to the newly opened White Castle burgers on the Vegas Strip. Earlier that night during the performance, Peter inserted the words "White Castle" into the lyrics of one of the songs to let me know he saw it. After the show, he came with us to revisit White Castle at 3:00 in the morning.

Since then, Peter Monroy and I have become friends and I try to make it over there from Los Angeles to see them perform as often as possible. It always turns out to be fun nights seeing such an awesome band perform live. He's an excellent front man with an amazing rapport with the audience. It took me several weeks, and it was like pulling teeth, but I finally got guitarist Kevin Woodall to show me some camera love.

What I find most interesting is, here is this cover band performing with no admission fee on Fremont Street in Vegas, and for most people it's their first visit to Vegas, yet with all there is to see and experience, they choose to stay and watch Spandex Nation for four prime nighttime hours. That says a lot for the band, especially when they are playing to bigger crowds than the original bands did when they were starting out.

This book is not about a typical performer making a stab at stardom as millions have in the past and will in the future only to see failure. This book is to document the journey of an extremely talented individual – the brainchild, leader, creator and astonishing vocalist of not one, but two continually working rock bands. Whether he reaches stardom status is yet to be seen, but his destiny is to become one of greatness, and his story should be known as one that gave it his all and will continue to do so in the future.

What truly sets apart Peter Monroy and the highly talented group of musicians that back him from others is the fact that they are not in one band – but two; the same band under different monikers, visual appearance and musical styles.

For many months, Frances had been boisterously talking about Spandex Nation with her fellow employees, especially when the weekend was fast approaching and we planned on attending one of their shows. The closer it came to our night out and to see the band, the more excited she became. She was constantly telling her co-workers that they should go to Fremont Street at night on the weekend to see one of the greatest 80's Hair Metal tribute bands that have ever graced the stage.

Then one Friday afternoon, a co-worker told Frances that he had seen one of the best bands to ever play on a stage at Fremont Street during the week. He bragged about their excellent musicianship and the wide variety of music they played. He described the band and she asked if their name is by any chance, Monroy. He said, "Yes... have you seen them?" Frances laughed, "Those are the same guys from Spandex Nation without their wigs."

I've worked with many bands in my past and have not seen a dedicated and hard working musician as Peter Monroy, the front man of Spandex Nation/Monroy.

Major headliners usually don't perform for more than two hours, and here you have a virtually unknown quartette of power players putting on a hard-driving, highly entertaining and energetic rock show for four late night hours, five nights a week and you rarely see them get tired. Neither extreme winter cold nor blazing hot desert heat can stop them from performing. That's because they don't view it as work... it's more about play time with the boys and performing music that they grew up with and dearly love as do the massive enthusiastic crowds that gather to watch them perform hit songs from Whitesnake, Bon Jovi, Ratt, Dokken, Cinderella, Skidrow, Motley Crue, Van Halen, Queensryche, Dio, AC/DC, Judas Priest, Iron Maiden, Autograph, Fastway, Van Halen, Def Leppard, Guns and Roses, Poison, Twisted Sister, Warrant, Quiet Riot and many more beloved 80's Metal bands. During those four hours, fans of that era of music are thrust into a leather, lace and spandex time machine and dropped smack dab in the middle of the Sunset Strip circa 1988.

Most of the original 80's bands are long gone, but their legacy lives on through bands such as Spandex Nation and Monroy whom is building their own massive fan base spanning across the globe. It is bands like Spandex Nation that are issuing in the re-birth of music that is fun, music with meaning that touches the soul and makes people feel alive – this is what 80's Hair Metal was. Everything cycles back around in due time... Welcome home Rockers!

Enjoy!   -Steven K Craig

Steven and Frances front row awaiting another blistering hot rock show by Spandex Nation.

Peter Monroy

Originally from Los Angeles, California, Peter Monroy is undoubtedly the hardest working, and one of the most talented, versatile vocalists in Las Vegas, Nevada.

His musical talent was apparent at a very young age. However, how could Peter not be so inclined and gifted being raised by a family of talent? His father was a classically trained tenor. He recognized his son's vocal talent and began coaching Peter to develop his unusual four-octave range. At the age of ten, Peter's flair for drums, guitar, and keyboards began to blossom. His love and ability to sing a vast range of music genres are far greater than that of the diverse radio stations in large metropolitan areas. Peter is now the driving force behind not one, but two critically acclaimed bands setting the bar for all others to follow on the Las Vegas show circuit.

As a teenager in 1984, Peter's love for hard rock and heavy metal took root as the local club scene, mainly the Sunset Strip, exploded with bands that would end up molding an entirely new genre of music that would last for many decades – Hardcore Metal, Speed Metal, Thrash Metal, Hair Metal, Glam Metal to name a few was coming out of the garage and into the mainstream. However, Peter was a couple years too young to gain entrance into the clubs to see the bands perform before they moved into large arenas. At fourteen years old, as Ratt was just becoming popular with their release of "Out of the Cellar", Peter was at home with his headphones on cranking songs at max volume of many other fast-rising groups that were about to be unleashed onto the unexpecting, frustrated, hormone induced youth that were primed and poised for the kill. One of his favorite virtually unknown bands at the time was Great White who had recently changed their name from Dante Fox. Peter sings with exuberance, "Bad Boy, I'm on the loose. I'm on the way... Bad Boy." Breaking from his vocal trance, Peter says, "Remember the song 'Stick It' from their first EP with the big middle finger on it? I recorded that song on eight-track tape."

He was unable to get into the 21 and over clubs where the bands were performing, but his friend James' mother would load them in her ever so cool van with chrome Centerline rims and an over-the-top Kenwood stereo that would induce bleeding from the ears and make the 45 minute trek to Reseda to see shows at the most famous hot spot for live music and debauchery, the Chuck Landis' Country Club (now the site of a church). She also took them to the Long Beach Sports Arena to see bands such as Iron Maiden. Peter adds, "That's how I got to see Ratt and Warrant. Funny thing, when I saw Warrant the first time, it looked like someone said (in a Middle Eastern accent), "The band is not here. These six rocker dudes, (pointing to nobody's in the crowd that just looked like rockers), bring them up and put them on the stage. Now get up there... here's a guitar." They were horrible. And then like two or three years later Janie Lane comes in, and it's awesome."

Shortly after, Peter began playing drums (one of his greatest loves). He purchased his first drum kit from Ron Albo who was in a band called Hostage. Hostage was an opening act for bands that were gaining regular rotation on Mtv such as Dokken and Ratt. He purchased the drum kit from Albo when Hostage self-imploded. He explains, "Their singer started getting on stuff (drugs) and showing up at gigs with guns and waving them at everybody. Everyone, including his band mates, were like, "Screw this... we're out of here." As much of a poor example of professional musicianship and reckless, destructive behavior as it was, this was the pivotal point that turned Peter on to that style of music and led him into becoming a musician. He put together his first band. As the "timekeeper" on drums, they wrote original music and performed at his high school.

Peter is blessed with an amazing gift of vocal ability. His father wanted him to sing. Frustrated at Peter's choice, he sternly said to Peter, "You are never going to make money playing the drums." But Peter was happy on his throne behind a drum kit.

In 1988, Peter relocated to the San Fernando Valley, California, just over the hill from Hollywood and the Sunset Strip. The Valley, yes the same place with the "Valley

Girls" that obliterated the English language with such phrases as "Fer Sher", which was also a hot spot for musicians and upcoming metal bands. He joined a band called "Shiro" which he says had an amazing guitar playing virtuoso similar to Yngwie Malmsteen.

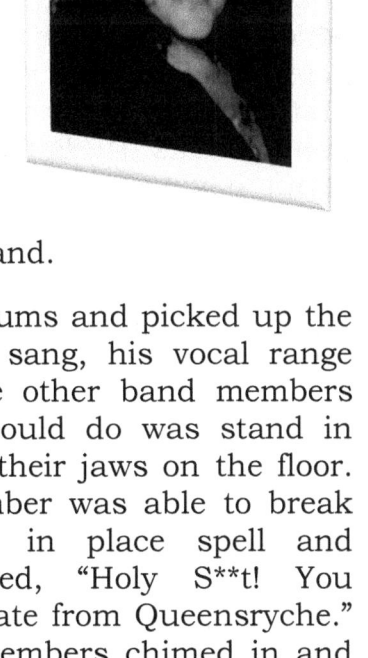

However, there arose immediate problems within the band as the singer was more focused on chasing women rather than being dedicated to practicing with the band.

Peter got off the drums and picked up the microphone. When he sang, his vocal range absolutely stunned the other band members and at first all they could do was stand in place, speechless with their jaws on the floor. Finally, one band member was able to break free from the frozen in place spell and enthusiastically shouted, "Holy S**t! You sound just like Geoff Tate from Queensryche." The remaining band members chimed in and said, "You sing from now on and we'll just get another drummer." New life was breathed into the band and all were anxiously excited to move forward. However, that was about to change.

Peter's father was extremely impressed with the growth of his vocals and he told Peter that he needed to record a demo tape. Dreams of his son becoming a successful performer filled his heart with joy. Peter's father and mother, along with a few mutual friends, decided to finance the band and collectively gathered the funds to put the band in a recording studio. They found a quaint little recording studio in Santa Barbara, California. The studio was equipped with a Linn drum kit which was one of the first electronic drum sets. Peter did it all from scratch and on his own at first. He played the drums and laid down guitar tracks. He laughed as he told the story about having to pretend there were cymbals with the electronic drums.

As the sessions progressed, Peter hired a few studio guitarists and turned it into a full-blown production by bringing in the producer of Cannibal and the Headhunters. Four songs were recorded, and Peter began sending the tapes out to everyone and anyone that had clout within the industry. A few months passed by without any interest, and then Peter received a phone call from Ron Oberman of CBS Records. Ron put Peter in touch with producer Tom Kelly. Tom was on the cutting edge and was looking for something outstanding. He was impressed with Peter and told him, "You have an amazing vocal ability. We just need to work on your material." As this was taking place, Peter became saved by Jesus and turned his life over to God. Tom made a few radical suggestions that would alter Peter's vision. Peter explains, "I wasn't going to sing about sticking this in your mouth and putting that down your throat." Peter's decision brought an abrupt halt to going any further with CBS. However, Peter assumed that if he obtained interest in a record contract from a major corporation so easily that he could get one in the Christian market just as easy, but time went on, and another deal was never offered.

Peter became a "born-again" believer in Christ and was on fire for God. He switched direction by forming a new band called JC Rocks and referred to themselves as "Musicianaries." Stepping away from the "all business" approach, they were able to have fun and thoroughly enjoying what they were doing. JC Rocks performed ant churches, and when they were not practicing of performing, the band went into the street to share the Gospel with kids on Hollywood Boulevard. They prayed with people on the Sunset Boulevard at the Troubadour (a hot spot for heavy metal bands) and were able to bring some of them to Jesus. That was not an easy task to do considering the mobs in front of the nightclubs mainly consisted of hardcore metal-heads that leaned more towards the dark side influenced by such local bands such as Slayer, W.A.S.P,

Hellion, Lizzy Borden, and Bondage themed bands such as Bitch.

Vigorously working together as a unit, the band wrote many original songs such as "Don't Stop Loving Me," "Forever and A Day" and "Party in Heaven." It wasn't long before JC Rocks ventured out into the church circuit and performed at mega-churches such as Pastor Chuck Smith's in Costa Mesa, California. "That place was huge," says Peter, "It was awesome! We got to sing for Jesus."

A few years before Peter formed JC Rocks, the Christian Metal band Stryper broke into the mainstream and achieved commercial success. Stryper gained immense popularity amongst the heavy metal fans due to the band's blistering catchy riffs and the non-metal crowd for the positive message they delivered. The band Holy Soldier was working their way up the ladder and Christian record labels were signing Iron Maiden versions such as Barron Cross and Mastodon. Peter had immense hope that his band JC Rocks would be able to follow in their footstep. However, JC Rocks had missed the signing spree and was never offered a recording contract.

On the home front, Peter's father was upset with him for his decision to give up the pursuit of becoming a Rock Star to follow Jesus and cut him off financially. He eventually got over being upset because any father that loved his children would want them to know God and Christ, but he forced Peter into getting a normal day job.

Timing is everything. It just so happened that at that same time, while Peter was working on bringing another musician into the fold of JC Rocks, a young drummer answered an advertisement Peter placed in Music Connection magazine. Music Connection magazine was based in Los Angeles, and its quarterly issues were loaded with music industry inside information and where serious musicians and industry personal connected with each other.

When the audition was over, the drummer asked Peter, "Hey, can you take me to my job interview?" Peter asked, "Hey, Do you think they will let me do an interview too?" Peter went with him and landed a job. Peter laughed when he said, "It was a Tele-Marketing" job. They will take anybody." Dreams of becoming a Rock Star were put on the back-burner, and he worked for the company for ten years from 1988 to 1998. Peter asserts that it wasn't a waste of time. He explains, "It was like boot camp for me. I didn't know it at the time, but later I would need to learn how to sell myself. That's what I learned during my tenure at the Tele-Marketing firm and what I do now – I sell myself."

During those ten years, Peter used the

extra money he earned to record music. He hired producers to assist him in developing a two and a half minute hit song. Peter struggled year after year to write what he believed would be a song that would launch his music career. It never came to fruition and in time it wore him out. Peter began to backslide. He started partying and chasing women. All his dreams came to an abrupt halt. For the time, his pursuit of music stardom was over.

Also, during that time period, Peter had reached the age that would allow him into the clubs on the Sunset Strip in Hollywood, but the local scene was changing. All the great Metal bands had been scooped up by record labels and were enjoying success in large arenas and receiving regular rotation on Mtv and world famous radio stations such as KNAC. Peter's musical taste shifted, and he elaborates, "I didn't know about bands such as Danger-Danger or Cinderella. Cinderella was kind of towards the tail end of where I was, and Metal had become too commercialized. Around 1989, after Skidrow, I kind of checked out of heavy metal music for awhile. I didn't want to hear bands such as Britney Fox because they were screwing it all up, and that's why by the early 1990's it was all over for me. I went to the black music like Dr. Dre, Snoop Dog, Warren G – that whole West Coast rap scene."

That phase was short lived. One of Peter's

musician friends informed him during a conversation that he was going to Las Vegas and was getting paid $1000 to sing. Peter was shocked, "What! Do you have any idea how many printer toner cartages I have to sell to make a thousand dollars?" Peter packed his bags and headed to Las Vegas. His mother was already living there along with the drummer from his old band Shiro. As soon as his feet hit the ground in Sin City, Peter got on the phone and called him, "I'm in Vegas. Let's get together and make a band." Peter spent a few weeks looking around Las Vegas and checking out the local music scene. Afterwards, he made the decision to stay and not return to Los Angeles.

Peter was fired up and jumped in with both feet. He was able to obtain a performance once a month. Once again, he was inspired to pursue his musical dreams and goals.

Scott, the drummer from Mr. Maccob, Kevin Woodall's old band, told him about this friend of his that he went to school with in Los Angeles; a singer that moved to Vegas and wanted to start a band. His name was Peter Monroy. Scott told Peter about Kevin. Kevin had just come off the road touring with a Country band. Peter was rather bewildered, "Country music?" But his friend informed him that Kevin absolutely loves Heavy Metal. Kevin Woodall is like a chameleon guitarist. He's a metal-head at heart, but has performed with Nat King Cole, and can play everything in-between covering a vast range of music genres.

They decided to meet in person and hit it off very well because both liked 80's metal. Peter explained to Kevin that he wanted to start a metal tribute band. That band would be called "Kid Hollywood". Scott also was interested in the project and decided to play drums in the band. All they needed was a bass player, and they would be set to go forward with the project.

Peter had three goals he wanted to accomplish right out of the gate, and Kevin became his teammate. The first priority for Peter was to record his original material that was of a Latin "adult contemporary" flavor in English similar to Celine Dion.

Peter thought to expand their play list and get into the casinos. Unable to rest due to his quest of succeeding, he formed the third band that would use his name as the moniker – The Peter Monroy Band.

They began playing Top 40 and Disco, and landed a five night a week gig at "Vacation Village" which was an older hotel/casino on the south end of the strip. It had a great lounge with an elevated stage and old Vegas style velvet curtains.

They remained at Vacation Village for 18 months until the casino closed. They tore the place down and put up a Fry's Electronics. The band then moved the show to the "Monte

They remained at Vacation Village for 18 months until the casino closed. They tore the place down and put up a Fry's Electronics. The band then moved the show to the "Monte Carlo" Casino and a few other locations. Then they ended up with a house gig at the "Paris" casino.

He put all three bands out onto the circuit at one time, and all three failed to gain any major interest. Peter was able to get one original song entitled "I'm the Only One" on a local AM radio station, and then nothing came of it. Peter completely enjoyed the 80's tribute

band called 'Kid Hollywood". Kid Hollywood performed all over Las Vegas. They performed Monday nights at the Boston, Thursday nights at what used to be called The Beach Club and then Saturday nights at Pinkies, but the band never made a dime. It was costing him money to operate the band and he decided to shut it down. From 1998 to 1999, Peter pushed those three projects with all he had in him but the only one that eventually began making money was the Peter Monroy Band. The Peter Monroy Band played a wide range of music styles from different genres and eras.

Peter was hanging out with two girls that worked at the Bellagio Hotel and Casino when one of them, his girlfriend at the time, recommended that he get a job playing at the Lounge in the Bellagio. He had not played a Lounge. He laughed out loud, "What am I going to play – Shout at the Devil by Motley Crue?" The girls suggested that he learn some pop songs that were all the rage the time. Sugar Ray was hot then and so was Kid Rock, Marl Anthony and at the top of the charts was Ricky Martin with "Livin' La Vida Loca".

Peter decided that the only way to land such engagements in high profile hotels was to produce a professionally recorded video to go along with his resume'. He quickly came up with an idea, got the money needed for production and shuttled the band to SIR Studios in Los Angeles.

"I always wanted to play SIR Studios", says Peter, "I used to go to showcases there to see other bands trying to get signed. I was so excited that we were actually going to be playing the place. We were there for three days. The Enrique Iglesias band members were there. I asked, "What are you doing here? They whispered, "Shhh.. we're moving furniture to look like we are busy. He (Enrique) hasn't been here for three days." They just moved stuff around to make it appear as they were doing something because they were getting paid for their time. This went on while we were

rehearsing to make the video."

The video didn't turn out as well as expected, but Peter hustled it regardless of its poor quality. He was desperate for a place to practice performing live. He grabbed a phone book and started calling every place he could find that had live music, many of which he had never heard of before. Out of 100 phone calls, only one showed interest. It was more like a dive-bar, but it was a place to perform. The property was owned by a couple of kids that decided to put up a small casino. The general manager returned Peter's call and offered him a two week contract. Peter was desperate and took the position. Peter rushed over to the casino in a business suit, "They didn't know what to think of me showing up dressed the way I was." After signing the contract, he rushed back and told Kevin Woodall that they needed to quickly put some songs together.

The band scrambled to put together a show in a style requested by the casino. Not in their repertoire, they needed to come up with something fast. They had only rehearsed seven songs similar to what the casino wanted. One band member said, "I know 'Brown Eyed Girl' and then another member knew a different song. Peter hired two young girls to sing songs and dance on stage as well, and together, they all made it work. Three days later they were performing on stage.

After a few days of performing, Peter was notified the owner wanted to see him. His initial thought was that the band blew it and was going to be fired. He was disappointed, "Oh man, we didn't even make it five days. I had a bad feeling this was going to happen with me having to sing oldies such as Lou Rawls' "You'll Never Find Another Love Like Mine." To Peter's surprise, the casino owner said, "We've been waiting for an act like you. We want to put you on TV. We want to offer you a year contract."

Peter thought to himself, "Is this really happening?" He hesitated on signing the contract as his ego began to take control. In his mind, he was thinking, "If this guy is all hard on us – imagine how the other casinos and clubs might be down on the Strip." At that point, Peter almost stopped listening to them.

Peter went back to the dressing room where Kevin was anxiously waiting. Concerned, he asked if they were fired. Peter replied, "No, they want to sign us for a year, and they want to make TV commercials and all this other stuff." Kevin asked, "Did you sign?" Peter replied with a solemn tone of voice, "No, I don't know if I want to sign." Kevin demanded, "You better sign it!"

Peter procrastinated, and problems arose before he could sign the deal. The club was providing rooms for the bands dancers from

Los Angeles to stay in during the period that the band would be performing at that location. All of a sudden, the management decided that the girls could no longer stay on the premises.

Peter was furious and got on the phone with the manager. He kept calm as he said, "You're offering me a year contract, and they need find a place to live. You cannot make them leave right now. The girls need at least 90 days to find a place to live." Peter was unable to make any headway and decided to fight back. In haste, he sent upper management an email that he was raising his price for the band to perform because they pissed him off. He wrote, "Now you've made me angry – I'm upping my price, and I want the girls to have rooms for the next year. That's it!" They called him on the phone within minutes and said, "You've got your two-week notice – you're out." Peter hung up the phone and mumbled, "Opps… that wasn't the response I was going for."

Before the Peter Monroy Band performed there, the club was a ghost town. The band was gaining popularity in town and the following weekend Monroy figured that they would go out in style by putting on the best show the casino has ever seen there.

Sunday morning, Peter was in bed, and his phone started ringing non-stop. He was groggy and yelled, "Who in the hell is this?" It was the general manager of the casino. He said, "Peter, we are so sorry. We want to sign your agreement. You got it!" Still half asleep, Peter calmly said, "Ok, thank you, bye."

However, when the problem arose, the casino wasted no time in trying to find a replacement band, and it just so happened that weekend of what the band thought would be their final performance there an agent came in wanting to bring her act there. When Peter pulled his "power-play", they offered her the spot.

Peter's band caught wind of the band that was there to take their spot as a weekend night-time headlining act. Together as a band, they decided to go see a day-time performance of this other band vying to take over their position. Peter didn't particularly want to go and showed up late. The band was on break. He sat with Kevin Woodall and their drummer at the time. Peter looked around the room and spotted his keyboard player talking to an amazingly beautiful blonde woman named Jennifer. He rushed over to where she was seated, and said in his best sexy, suave voice that he could muster up, "Hey, how are you doin'?" She shot Peter down in a ball of flames, and he walked away with his tail between his legs.

Peter returned to his band-mates as the other band took to the stage. Peter was floored when he found out that they sexy woman that just blew him off is also the singer of the band that is after his job.

Jennifer Halloway performing at the Tropicana in Las Vegas. Breaking News! The secret is out. For those of you familiar with the Howard Stern show, this is the same Jennifer Halloway made famous on the show that was sung about in a song that has been played many times in the past.

Jennifer had no idea of who Peter was or the problem that had occurred with his contract. All said and done, both bands ended up performing together at the casino. She did her shows during the day, and the Peter Monroy Band did theirs at night.

Peter was fascinated with Jennifer, and he continued to hit on her for days. He invited her to many places such as the Eifel Tower, and she continued to shoot him down by rejecting his offers. Peter, being a ladies' man, could only assume that Jennifer was going out with some boisterously wealthy geek because she wanted nothing to do with the likes of him – a performer struggling to make it.

She was driving Peter crazy, and he decided to step up his game. He went to the casino early before his band was scheduled to arrive and invaded the dressing room by walking in unannounced before Jennifer had a chance leave. Peter paid no attention to the fact that he might be unwelcome because it was his place as well and he figured that he ran the place. Jennifer was thinking, "Oh my gosh... who is this person?" Peter nonchalantly seated himself alongside her and whispered, "Apparently dinner is out of the question... so, how about lunch? I can't do anything to you at lunch, during the day, surrounded by millions of people."

Finally, she agreed to meet him for lunch, and they chose PF Chang's the following day. However, with his head in the clouds, Peter completely forgot that he had to take his parents to the airport that day which would conflict with his and Jennifer's date. Peter frantically rushed to be on time, but he was thirty minutes late. Jennifer was mere moments from leaving as Peter rushed into the restaurant. Looking back now, they both thank God that she didn't leave.

There's may not be exactly a Cinderella story, but Peter and Jennifer have both found their love of a lifetime. Peter and Jennifer have been together ever since. They eventually got married and now they have an awesome son named "Rock". However, before any of that took place, the casino closed down, and the band needed to find new employment.

Peter quickly landed a full-time position performing at the Venetian Hotel and Casino in its main lounge. During his ten year run at the Venetian, the Peter Monroy Band gained local acclaim and became a staple of the Las Vegas music scene. However, after a few years into it, Kevin Woodall parted ways with Peter and went onto another project.

During his time at the Venetian, Peter recorded an EP of originals. The general manager there was very supportive of his original music. He especially liked Peter's record called, "Level Seven", which was about him not being able to deal with the politics of music. The only way he found to be able to cope with the stress was to smoke (marijuana) every moment he possibly could. Peter would go on his breaks to the upper level 7 parking lot and just smoke his brains out, and then go back down and put on a remarkable performance. He did this day after day and every time he got in and out of the elevator, he saw the sign in bold red letters reading "Level 7" That is how the title of his EP came to be. It should have been the happiest time of his life, but turned out to be one of the most miserable. Finally, one day he woke up, and he knew that he had to pull it together before it all collapsed on him.

Then good things began to happen for Peter. The Venetian hired a new sound engineer for his band, and when Peter found out, it reignited the flame inside him that was the driving force behind his love for music. Peter ended up learning from the new head of sound. Angelo Arcuri produced and engineered Ronnie James Dio's "Holy Diver", "Last in Line" and "Dream Evil" albums. Peter is a huge Dio fan, and this new union gave him inspiration and made him feel blessed. Peter adds, "It's amazing how many talented people that I've been able to work with from that era."

After signing a contract with the Venetian, Peter received many perks. The television show "Americas Got Talent" used the premises to film part of its auditions. Peter's boss at the Venetian used his pull to get Peter an audition. Peter didn't want to do it, but his boss demanded, "Get in there! You've got to do this. Come on... you want to be a star, don't you?" Peter didn't care. He was happy with where he was in life. He was making good money. He had a girlfriend that he loved dearly (Jennifer, before they were married). They were having a great time together. Sometimes they would be out all night until nine o'clock in the morning and then sleep all day until they went back out at night to perform. Peter couldn't care any less about the audition. His head wasn't in the right place for it, but to appease his boss, he had the band dress like the boy band 'N Sync and went onstage to perform Motley Crue's "Live Wire". Peter threw his hands in the air and yelled into the microphone, "Thank you – Goodnight!", and then he walked out. The staff of Americas Got Talent shook their heads in disbelief. Looking at each other, one said, "What in the hell was that? Is that what the Venetian sent over here?"

In 2011, Peter started to think that the fact he was getting older that he had better do something soon. America's Got Talent came back, and they (Venetian) requested that he do the audition again. The manager from the

Venetian paid for everything. He was very close to the producers of the show, and he saw another opportunity to get Peter on the show. He took Peter out to Los Angeles for the audition. Peter went in and took it seriously this time, but didn't get past the first audition.

Peter refused to give up and without the help of the Venetian; he went out his own to the next talent show audition making its way through the West Coast.

Peter and Jennifer went to Los Angeles and stayed at his sister's house. At 4:30 in the morning, they stood in the pouring rain with 15,000 people at the Sports Arena that were also in line for The X-Factor. Peter was set on giving it his all this time. When his turn came, Peter got onstage and sang "Don't Stop Believing" by Journey and he gave them a sad story because they love that stuff. Peter had no scruples at that moment and told them a heartbreaking story. Peter made it past the first round of auditions, got the golden ticket and ran through the crowd to tell Jennifer the good news. Peter called his band that was waiting in Las Vegas to hear what news he had for them and he told them that they will need to postpone their upcoming shows because he would be staying in Los Angeles.

Peter got through another round of auditions, and then he was told that he was going to be put in OG. Puzzled at first and then

> **CONGRATULATIONS!**
> You have made it through to the next stage of
> THE X FACTOR 2011.
>
> Please take this slip and make your way to the YES Room.
> There you will be given the date and time for your next audition.
>
> **YOU MUST NOT LOSE THIS SLIP**
> YOU WILL NOT BE ABLE TO CONTINUE IN THE COMPETITION
> WITHOUT IT!

Peter is told, "It's the Older Group." At that moment, Peter felt as if he was truly old. In his own words, Peter explains what happened next, "I had to go through these other producers before I would get to see Simon Cowell. There were so many producers in there and I thought, "What am I going to do? I got to blow them away. I'm going to do a Led Zeppelin medley right there and annihilate them. So they call my name, I walk into the room and I'm all nervous thinking I might really get onto television. This is going to help me so much and my family. I asked, "Where are the executives?" The last time I did an audition like this it was for CBS, which is now Sony, and in a meeting, there were older guys in suits that looked like bad-asses, and this time and its two skater dudes - two young kids in hoodies. I'm looking around for the executives and then realize... the two kids were them. I did Led Zeppelin and they were like, "Oh... That's awesome. Hey man, can you Rap?" I can Rap, but I told them that I can't because I didn't want to start Rapping on TV. I didn't feel as if that's what I wanted to be famous for. Was it a mistake? Maybe I should have just rapped and could have got on the show and possibly got to turn it a different direction afterwards, but I didn't."

In 2013, Peter auditioned for The Voice which is the most popular talent show on television. Peter was disappointed with the auditions. After he sang, Peter was told that he needed singing lessons. Ironic is it not that Peter has gained global fame for his vocal ability? The Voice continues to send Peter invitations to audition again, but he says that he refuses to play their game. Peter explains, "I know some people go on it two, three, four times before they make it. That's not for me. I'm not a teenager any longer. I have a family to support and you can't work in-between their shows. Winning those shows don't really matter because most of the winners end up here in Vegas as Lounge Acts and I've already moved beyond that."

During his stay at the Venetian, the Peter Monroy Band continued to gain popularity and was changing the direction of things to come in the near future concerning live music in Las Vegas. An article in a local magazine wrote that Monroy has given a much needed facelift in mega-proportions to live music on the Vegas Strip.

When he began his residency, the norm was bands performing songs such as "Stand by Me" with the members wearing Bermington coats and the same color suits – blue, red or gold. It was too polished and what was expected from a Las Vegas lounge act circa 1965. There was no Hard Rock music to be found anywhere. Peter was auditioning at the New Orleans and busted loose with a Motley Crue song. An assistant manager came down and said, "That was awesome, but don't let the general manager hear that. You'll be fired immediately." Always thinking about marketing, Peter wondered if he could make the newspaper for being fired for playing heavy metal in a casino and if it would be great publicity.

Peter was just trying to be himself and do the music he loves most. Steve Via Productions sent upcoming musicians over to see the Peter Monroy Band perform. Steve instructed, "Go see Monroy; that's how a rock and roll show is supposed to be done. Peter paved the way to make it okay to do screaming vocals and hard rock/heavy metal in a five star, six diamond hotel.

When former NBA star Dennis Rodman was in town to celebrate his 50th birthday, he joined Peter on stage.

Kevin Woodall was working with an R&B and Rap band called "Atomic Milkshake". They were a very fun party band and had a weekly gig at "Treasure Island" casino and hotel.

It had been a few years since Kevin had seen Peter Monroy, and since the Venetian was right across the street, Kevin would walk over on his break to watch him perform. They began talking again and rekindled their friendship.

During Peter's tenure at the Venetian, the hotels lounge was in the red when he began and was in the black when he moved on. Peter was instrumental in making it cool to like hard rock from the 1980's in a big hotel casino. Afterwards, they continued by bringing in the Rock of Ages show into the Bourbon Room.

Once Peter felt that he reached his peak at

the Venetian with the Peter Monroy Band, he decided it was time to move on to greener pastures and to do something new that could propel him forward. They attempted to sign on with Caesars Palace because they own eight properties. He played a couple shows but they turned out to be a horrible experience. The staff was extremely mean and treated them like garbage.

Peter made the decision to take his band Downtown to Fremont Street. Fremont is a major hot spot for live music and has three outdoor stages within walking distance of each other. Many well-known superstar bands spanning several decades make appearances on a Fremont Street stage. The shows are free to the tens of thousands of nightly visitors. This is the place for a band to be seen and generate fans worldwide.

At that time, he was also playing rhythm guitar in an AC/DC production show and continued on with it. This is when Kevin met Ryan Gillian.

Then one day, Kevin received a call from Peter Monroy. He wanted to know if Kevin would be willing to perform at a few shows with him as a substitute guitar player. Kevin had the time to do it, so he agreed to do it. Kevin knew Peter had a night downtown on Fremont Street, and that the band didn't like the guitar player they had. They liked Kevin, and wanted him to stay with the band. He liked them as well and took the position. Kevin completed his contract with the AC/DC show, and then Peter and he joined forces once again.

After a month or so performing on Fremont Street., they were playing a few 80's rock songs from their "Kid Hollywood" days. The head soundman wanted to know if they would put together an 80's Rock Tribute Show. Of course that was their first love. And so began the second incarnation of Kid Hollywood which later became Spandex Nation.

Ryan Gillian was brought onboard as the drummer. Ryan was an excellent fit for the band since he is a power hitter and likes to rock.

Peter shortened the name of the band to just Monroy and with Kevin Woodall back on guitar the band was given new life. Now at the helm of sound engineering was a guy that worked for Ratt and the band sounded better than they ever had before, and better yet, a second sound engineer named Joe Pizzo came it and pushed it over the top. Peter became excited again due to the strong thunderous sound of the band on stage. On Fremont Street, bands perform four hour long sets with a fifteen minute break ever hour on the hour for the light show overhead on the dome. During a break, the sound engineer came back stage and said, "You guys do the heavy rock stuff very well. Can you make a band doing just that style of music?" Peter looked over at Kevin with a smirk on his face. He said, "Woody – Kid Hollywood – Next week." Kevin simply replied, "Done!" However, Peter and Kevin needed different members other than those in Monroy to complete the band for look and sound as it differed from that of Monroy.

In came Freddie Paguio (Doctor Rock) on bass and vocals and Ryan Gillian on drums. Kid Hollywood would be an 80's Hair Metal tribute band that celebrated the heyday of the Sunset Strip in Los Angeles with music by bands such as Ratt, Dokken, Judas Priest, Iron Maiden, Queensryche, Motley Crue, Guns and Roses just to name a few. To make the show complete the band needed to transform themselves by going back in time to dress the part and put on wigs of long flowing "big" hair.

Kid Hollywood (left to right) Ryan Gillian, Freddie Paguio, Kevin Woodall Peter Monroy.

Six weeks later, September 14th, 2014, Kid Hollywood was up and running once again and debuted on the First Street stage.

The second incarnation of Kid Hollywood became an instant hit on Fremont Street. The band was welcomed with open arms by fans of feel-good positive heavy metal music from the 1980's. People of all ages, young and old from around the world ate it up. Parents that loved these songs when they were young had their children with them whom sang along with the lyrics. Music that is old became new again.

Peter then decided to have Kid Hollywood perform at other venues around Las Vegas, but didn't receive the same warm welcome.

The band performed at "Vinyl" in the Hard Rock Casino; a place that one would think the band would draw a huge crowd, but didn't. Even thought the Hard Rock casino's theme revolves around Rock & Roll music with musical instruments from top selling artists strung throughout the building, there is not a large flow of people traffic. Peter reflects back to that night, "I watched people walking by as I was singing at Vinyl. There was a really big sign that said Kid Hollywood out front and they would miss as they walked by the front of the door. I imagine some of them thinking, "Is Kid Hollywood a cross dressing transvestite? Is it a boxer or a rapper? Is it a kid's band – what is it?"

That's when Peter realized he needed a name that would best represent his brand and started searching for a new name for the band. The next day, Peter was talking to his wife Jennifer and made a comment about loving the heavy metal station on Sirus radio called "Hair Nation" They had a sound byte that screamed and carried a long ending note, "Hair Natiooon!" and he loved the way it sounded. It was catchy and a tag line that just sticks in your head. Peter and Jennifer were bouncing ideas off each other and he made the remark, "Hair Nation's introduction say's it all. I need a name like that." Peter was in the shower. His eyes closed to keep the shampoo from getting in them. He and Jennifer were tossing ideas around, Hair this and Hair that... Spandex this and that, when Jennifer brainstormed, "Honey, why don't you use just use the name Spandex Nation?" Peter flung open the shower door, stepped out dripping wet with a huge smile on his face. He grabbed his wife and kissed her, saying, "That's it! I love it!" He loudly sang out, "Spandex Natiooooon" carrying the last note as high pitched and as long as he could project the air from his lungs. It excited him even more and he knew in his heart that would launch the band in the right direction.

When he officially changed the name from Kid Hollywood to Spandex Nation, it was not met with his same enthusiasm. In fact, many people did not like it and some fans gave Peter hell for the change. Even the staff of Fremont Street was not happy with the change. They said it was cheesy and would hurt the band. Months later, as the band continued to grow in popularity and the crowds became larger while the sound of Peter singing, "Spandex Natiooon" reverberated throughout the under-dome of Fremont Street, one of the executives that originally disagreed with the name change, told Peter, "When I'm wrong, I admit it, and I was wrong. Spandex Nation is brilliant. Everyone is singing it in the office. It's just incredible."

There are three stages located on Fremont Street. Spandex Nation was playing on the Third Street stage which is located in the center with the most people traffic and is the best stage for drawing in a crowd. Spandex Nation was drawing such a large crowd that executives decided to move them to the Main Street stage located at the end of Fremont. The Main Street stage was floundering and due to its location, the stage was unable to neither draw in nor hold a crowd there. The casinos next to the stage where suffering by not bring the patron their direction. Before moving the band to the Main Street Stage, one of the executives of Fremont Street had the stage update with a new sound and lighting system (even a smoke machine) to support Spandex Nation and provide the band with a place to put on a well produced Rock and Roll show. The gamble paid off for everyone connected with the move and production. Spandex Nation has been able to draw in thousands of nightly visitors to watch them perform.

Peter's vision, hopes and dreams are beginning to come to fruition and he's has been able to pull off what was once impossible. Dedication and drive will always triumph. Never done before in the history of Fremont Street that had a rule of a musical act only allowed performing one night a week, Peter has secured five nights a week through a combination of his two completely different bands, Monroy and Spandex Nation.

Now, the man that was once told he needed singing lessons has been named "The Voice of Fremont Street. Two bands, although different, have an amazing drawing power with crowds.

Two Rock Bands – One Incredible Talent.

Spandex Nation

Thirty years have passed since the peak of the Heavy Metal scene in Hollywood, California on the Sunset Strip. Time is taking its toll as the Metal Warriors of yesteryear are fading away, getting old, and some have already left this earth. However, their legacy lives on thanks to talented musician and diehard fans that span several generations.

The members of Spandex Nation are just that – musicians and fans of 80's metal that are paying tribute to the bands that influenced their career. "Performing these songs brings my fans back to the days when the hair was big and the music was bigger." – Peter Monroy

Hollywood was once the breeding ground for rock stars, but it is now a ghost town where musicians seeking success, fame and fortune have all but completely vanished. The majority of the famous rock palaces from the 80's are no longer. Buildings that were once shrines to music of all types have disappeared or hidden from plain view. Concert Row in Anaheim (Woodstock Concert Theater, Radio City and French Quarter) where bands such as Slayer, Metallica and Great White began their careers has been torn down and replaced with a strip Mall. The Golden West Ballroom where Van Halen launched their career is now a church. Gazzarri's was torn down, and the Reseda Country Club has been converted to a church as well. Another rock palace turned into a church? I wonder if the congregations of those converted buildings have any clue about that sex, drugs and rock & roll that took place within those establishments. Some remain such as the Troubadour and Whisky a Go Go, but those clubs that used to have long lines and hordes of long-haired rockers, fans and sexy women dressed to kill have no visible sign of life.

With Los Angeles, which used to be the music capital of the world a virtual music graveyard, where do serious musicians striving to pave their way to fame go? They head east to Las Vegas, which now holds the crown of the music/entertainment capital. However, to make it in Las Vegas, the musicians must be far above average – they must be the best of the best to make it. The days of the "overnight success" is basically a thing of the past, and the musicians now have to pay their dues by working extremely hard. This also means they must throw themselves out there in every direction possible to be seen and heard. Many Las Vegas musicians are not just part of one band but several at one time. It's reminiscent of the theory about throwing it all out there and see what sticks. However, this leads to one problem – which is life. And with life comes problems such as paying the bills. Many musicians in Las Vegas see performing as a job just for a paycheck and do not possess the ambition and dedication for major success. And then there are those that want it but are forced to leave performing to support their family. Both of which has hampered Peter from reaching his destiny of stardom sooner than later.

A few months into the project, Ryan had to leave the band. Ryan had many personal responsibilities outside the band and a good paying job with benefits. He was unable to commit to more than one to two nights a week, and both parties thought it would be for the best if the band sought a more permanent solution.

At the same time, Freddie Paguio had to

leave the band as well. He works as head of valet at the Wynn Casino and was not able to work multiple nights a week on Fremont Street. He was recently married and was making a good living at the Wynn and had a great benefits package and couldn't jeopardize losing it.

Peter Monroy and Freddie Paguio

As luck may have it, when it looked as if the band was in trouble, another band in town had just disbanded and the musicians were looking for a new gig.

It just so happened that the drummer and bassist from Marigold, Daniel Patrick Conway and Kevin Vecchione, were able to step in and fill the slots to keep the mighty machine working without missing a heartbeat.

(Above)-Fourth of July, 2015

Monroy

Taking you on a musical journey through the 70s 80s and current hits along with original songs, Monroy is a live performance not to be missed.

Monroy has the band appearing as

themselves in street clothes and performing popular songs of many genres and several decades of music.

The band as a unit is very tight and has the ability to replicate cover songs well enough to please even the most critical of fans. The Monroy band is more than able to execute with precision songs from Pharrell to Snoop Dog, Lou Rawls, Boston and Led Zeppelin. They perform everything popular from Metallica to Michael Jackson and do so four hours a night, two nights a week. The Monroy Show takes fans on a musical journey through the '70's, '80's, '90's up to current hits of today. As one audience member put it, "No matter what age you are, there's a song for everybody!" Wednesday and Thursday night, thousands of people are treated to a show that is truly one that is the Rock of Ages. Monroy has developed a strong and loyal fan base called MONROCKERS, both from travelers to Vegas and hometown regulars. Peter commented, "Monroy is a classy band. Not saying that Spandex isn't, but sometimes it's okay to be a little trashy."

Come Friday night, the band puts on their wigs resembling the long locks of those young hero's of the golden era of big Hair Metal. Off goes the everyday street clothes and on come the spandex, leather, lace and spikes – and onstage struts the Rock God's of Vegas "Spandex Nation" to perform four hours of classic and beloved metal tunes from the 1980's. Older people get to relive the glory days of what took place on the Sunset Strip in Hollywood, California, and the young kids today get to experience it themselves for the first time. It's a heavy metal show that can be seen again and again because the band is always adding new songs and rotating others throughout their weekly performances. Peter says, "I want all the cover songs Spandex Nation does to sound killer, and I don't want anybody to leave the show disappointed."

Peter is not just a performer or an actor onstage. When the wig and outfit goes on, he becomes Kid Hollywood. Just as Vincent Furnier stated, when the makeup goes on, he is no longer himself, he becomes Alice Cooper. Peter says, "Kid Hollywood is me. But there is still part of me there, obviously because I'm soft-spoken." There is a noticeable difference between Peter on stage as himself (Monroy), and Kid Hollywood (Spandex Nation), his body movements, attitude, personas are completely different. As Kid Hollywood, he is a larger than life Rock Star.

Peter Monroy is at the helm of Spandex Nation and Monroy, but he wouldn't be where he is now without his longtime partner of over seventeen years, Kevin Woodall. Other band members have come and gone, but these two are truly a team, kind of like Gene Simmons and Paul Stanley from KISS.

Kevin is soft spoken and has a kind and

gentle disposition... that is until he hits the stage and transforms into a metal guitar god as his fingers aggressively shred the fretboard on his trusty white Gibson SG battleaxe producing riffs so hot that they could ignite a blazing inferno.

Both bands, Spandex Nation and Monroy are at this time reaping their rewards for staying dedicated to their craft, and the band members are fully enjoying their time in the limelight. After playing nearly every club and casino in Las Vegas, the band hit pay-dirt by landing a contract with Fremont Street, which is the best showplace in town. Kevin is delighted, and says, "I always tell everyone that Fremont Street is the best people watching spot in Las Vegas, and of course, we have the best view in the house. We can see almost everything from the stage. At some point, it seems everyone visiting Las Vegas strolls through Fremont Street at one time or another. I love meeting new fans and people from all over the globe. A recent Fourth of July, the lead singer and guitar player from the band LIT was hanging out and wanted to sit in with us, so they came up and we played their hit song "My Own Worst Enemy". Earlier that year, we played an afternoon show to promote a new booze and a new record for Sammy Hagar. Sammy, Jason Bonham, and Michael Anthony all came up on stage and jammed a little."

It's true that all bands develop hardcore fans, and some even go beyond attending performances. There are those that believe so wholeheartedly in a band and their music that they will dedicate their time in helping to promote the band. These people are the steam that keeps the engine running smoothly. For Spandex Nation, one of those people is Patti Hodder.

Patti travelled consistently for many years to Las Vegas setting up trade shows for her company. During the summer of 2008, Patti and her co-workers were walking through the Venetian Hotel and Casino when she heard an amazing rendition of Bon Jovi's "Dead or Alive". For a split second, she thought that Bon Jovi was performing somewhere in the hotel. She followed the sound, and it led her to an open lounge on the casino level. She was even more surprised when she found there was no admission fee. Patti and her friends shimmied their way through the thick crowd and found one of the few remaining tables that were still available to be seated.

For the next hour, they were transfixed by this amazing band. They covered every genre of music and that band was tight! As they were watching, Patti realized that the lead singer was wearing her company's shoes. When the band took a break, they basically accosted the lead singer and explained who they worked for. He nicely introduced himself and proceeded to show them that his entire wardrobe was her company's products – from his shoes to his jacket and briefcase. They explained who we worked for and he indulged those crazy New Yorkers throughout the rest of his set.

Peter is without a doubt one of the nicest people/musicians anyone could meet. He is soft spoken and always polite, on and off stage.

As the night ended, Patti asked him what his shoe size was and, much to his surprise, he was considered a sample size. She promised to come back with some shoes for him. Although he was extremely sweet to them, Patti did think he thought she was completely full of shit.

But, the next night went back to his show with two shopping bags stuffed with shoes and that is when their friendship began.

Patti continued to attend Peter's shows on each trip out to Vegas and in addition to footwear, her job expanded to include men's apparel. She was able to hook Peter up with cool clothing and accessories and what was great about this arrangement was his sincere gratitude with everything he ever received. Some people view rock stars as pompous, self-absorbed, but what always impressed Patti about Peter was a great talent combined with a great man.

Throughout the years although the band line-up and venues changed, what remained the same was Peter's talent and devotion to his family, friends and fans.

When he had the opportunity to expand his presence on Fremont Street with Spandex Nation, Patti was in town and got to go wig shopping with him. She says, "That was a blast! And I recommended some fabric for his headbands and found vintage rock t-shirts and cut them up to look like what we remembered from back in the day."

Life changes and Patti was let go from her job. She picked herself up and started her own company. Peter and her were discussing things and he was mentioning that he just couldn't keep up with the demands and necessity of social media platforms. Patti said, "Hey, I can help". So now, with his direction, Patti manages his social media presence and developed websites for both bands, including e-commerce and promo items for his fans.

Over the past seven years, Patti had the great pleasure of starting out as a fan, becoming a friend and now a business partner. She adds, "Peter's dedication to his music and his fans is 100% authentic and I am proud to be a part of Monroy and Spandex Nation. We continue to discuss new ways to involve his fans and developed PERISCOPE broadcasts and are working on t-shirts and other items to get into the hands of his fans worldwide. I am excited to see what's next for Peter and his bands – he works incredibly hard and deserves the best."

Peter is seeing the light at the end of the tunnel. Instead of giving up attempting to break into one of the most difficult industries to succeed or perform in smoke-filled bars getting paid barely enough to put gas in their vehicle to make the round trip, they work as, not one, but two cover bands and perform to thousands of people a night on stage at one of the most prime locations in Las Vegas. On those nights, he becomes a superstar. Not willing to give up his pursuit of musical success, he continues to push forward until the day comes that he gets his big break.

What's in the future for Spandex Nation? One might think that due to the success of Steel Panther (originally an 80's metal cover band) that Spandex Nation would try to follow in their footsteps. That would be a fatal error for the band as it's already been done. Peter adds, "I would like nothing more than to be like Motley Crue, wild and all, but times have changed. Our shows are not 21 and over, I almost never curse while performing. Sometimes there is a slip of the tongue and I'm sorry when that happens. There are other bands out there that have no problem with, "Hey man, it's the grand opening." "Of what man?" "Her vagina!" I don't have stuff like that in my show. Peter whispers, "Because I'm not good at it. It's also not my thing (he laughs). Steel Panther makes fun of the whole thing (genre) and you won't find me doing that. Not that what they are doing is bad because they are funny and they are really good at it, but that's not my style. I'm not funny like that. However, I am proud of the fact that anybody can come to our show."

Peter is working on setting Spandex Nation in a direction that will bring back the sound of the 80's heavy metal. He is constantly writing new music. Peter explains, "I want us to become bigger than Steel Panther with our own originals. It's tough to emulate the music of that time with the same feel. Music has changed. Those beloved choruses have become like nursery rhymes. Song writing has changed. I try to write with the times but I keep going back to that awesome anthem style of choruses."

Peter is also working on taking Monroy to the next level by writing original material. He knows deep in his soul that that hit song is inside him, and one day, it will come out for all to hear.

He concludes, "I love the band. We love travelling together. I love being around them. I do want to take it to the next level, and I hope God is working on it. I just want to be faithful to Him, my family, our business and whatever else comes our way.

Visit Peter's Websites:

www.spandexnation1.com

www.petermonroy.com

For More Books by Steven K Craig

www.steven-k-craig.com

www.ingramcontent.com/pod-product-compliance
Lightning Source LLC
Chambersburg PA
CBHW060410050426
42449CB00009B/1942